VOICES AGAINST SILENCE

ALAN HOLDER

for Rosanna,

the center of my *vita nuova*

VOICES AGAINST SILENCE

ALAN HOLDER

ANAPHORA LITERARY PRESS

ATLANTA, GEORGIA

Anaphora Literary Press
1803 Treehills Parkway
Stone Mountain, GA 30088
http://anaphoraliterary.com

Book design by Anna Faktorovich, Ph.D.

Cover Images: "Rocky Ring of Debris Around Vega." NASA. Huntingdon Institute for X-ray Astronomy/G. Garmire, Optical: ESO/VLT.

Published in 2014 by Anaphora Literary Press

Voices Against Silence
Alan Holder—1st edition.

ISBN-13: 978-1-937536-86-2
ISBN-10: 1-937536-86-6

Library of Congress Control Number: 2014950750

CONTENTS

OTHER BOOKS BY ALAN HOLDER

Three Voyagers in Search of Europe: A Study of Henry James, Ezra Pound and T.S. Eliot
A.R. Ammons
The Imagined Past: Portrayals of Our History in Modern American Literature
Rethinking Meter: A New Approach to the Verse Line

Chapbooks

Opened: A Mourning Sequence
Aging Head in the Clouds

ACKNOWLEDGMENTS

Some of these poems originally appeared in the following publications:

Adirondack Review
Timber Creek Review
Ibbetson Street
The Café Review
Thorny Locust
Jewish Currents
Lilliput Review
Shofar
Avalon Literary Review

AGAINST SILENCE

If you think silence is golden,
try visiting a class of four-year-olds,
lingering a bit in the room just after
they have left, and see if you enjoy
the dense absence of their voices.

What terrified Pascal was not the size
of interstellar spaces but their eternal
silence. Rightly so—keeping its mouth
shut, the cosmos is the ultimate
withholder, refusing us comfort
or direction—mum's the word.

So why the celebration of silence
in poems, in discourse about music,
in monasteries or on weekend retreats?

We were made to speak—
even in silent reading (what you
are presumably doing right now),
our throat muscles are at work
in subliminal articulation, yearning
to turn every word into a speech act.

For all their failures or limitations,
with each of the words we utter,
we have hurled a tiny, defiant spear
against our shared, mute abyss.

FORECAST: SEVERE THUNDERSTORMS

Here come Heaven's strobe lights, flashes
delivered in slimmest slivers of time,
each a rip, a seam, a sky-scar,
gone almost as soon as it appears.

It's not those bolts that make us jump,
but their laggard attendants,
showily announcing the cracking
apart of the world-dome–what else
could it be?—Will it fall on our heads?—
we flinch without shame.

The storm moves on, rumbling,
muttering, grouchy in its departure
over not having been allowed,
for all its display of lumens and decibels,
to put us beyond all seeing, all hearing.

HIGH WIND ALERT

The high wind alert today has certainly worked
for me. Rarely have I been more alert than I am
right now, as I stand outside, watching
the trees made to bend this way, then that, this way,
then that. The beech has already surrendered
two great branches, and I am afraid for other trees,
for the garden fence, the car, the barn, the house.
The very order of things seems as if it could be
uprooted, blown away.

But suddenly the trees are masts, stripped
of their sails—it is late autumn—the earth
all around me a million-masted vessel
adrift as always on the high seas of space,
buffeted as always by galactic winds,
rained on as always by primeval particles.

Even on halcyon days, we are rooted only
in motion, anchored only in quantum leaps,
awash with ceaseless waves of energy.
There is no tiller, no compass, no destination,
there is only our attention, to give or not,
only self-alertings to what is there and what is not.

FROM SECOND TO SECOND

That I was able to get from word to word
in writing this, that you are able to get
from word to word in reading it,
is courtesy of God, says Jonathan Edwards—
God has not simply created the universe
and set it in motion. No—He wills
its continuance from second to second,
a thrilling idea (if you buy it), charging
every instant of our lives with God's assent,
whether we be sneezing, going to the toilet,
or looking at the stars, themselves
dependent on God's saying again and again
"Let the stars continue to be for the next second."

That's one way of looking at it.
Another is to see the universe as hard-wired
to have things continue as they have been going,
so that wherever we find ourselves will be
there the next second, and we will,
for better or worse, be carried alive
through any given day and any given night,
awaking on the beds in which we went to sleep.
This view puts our trust in a Newton-like law:
A body in existence tends to continue
in existence, God or no God.

But there is evidence for yet another view,
that there is, in the nature of things, a gap
between any two moments, whose width
may be inconsequential, or of sufficient size
to allow a fatal fall, a stroke, an aneurysm,
a crash, a cell wildly multiplying,
a gun gone off by accident, an IED
gone off by design, a person become a bomb.
A body in existence tends to continue in existence—
or not.

BIRDING

My favorite bird? I'm glad you asked.
It used to be the blue jay, that cock
of the walk, uncaring,
in its knockout outfit, that it can't
sing but only ripsaw the air
with brilliant screechings.

Next came the nuthatch,
descending tree trunks at a headlong
trot, as if it has forgotten how to fly
and had better get down to terra firma
just as quickly as it can.

After that came the crow,
coal –black giant of the low flyers,
skittish as anything when on the ground,
but never, once in the trees, afraid to scream
"Here I am, turkey," gathering with its kind
in crowds of cacophony to scare off predators
or maybe just for the hell of it, declaring
the charms of silence much overrated.

But now my feathered darling is the yellow finch,
which comes to the feeder partly
for occasional jabs at the sunflower seeds,
but mainly, it seems, to hang out,
chirp softly, look around,
contemplate the nature of things,
giving us the pleasure of its plump brilliance

If this be a birdbrain, so be it.

BEYOND AUDOBON

I

Trapped in the decrepit office at the top
of the barn, undoubtedly crazed by enclosure,
it blundered its way behind a wall,
pecked a hole in the sheetrock, poked its head through,
and stuck.

I've rescued several of its kind
from that room, seen them—speckled, iridescent, frantic—
only there, never in the bushes, trees,
or *Peterson's Guide*, but this one
was dead on my arrival,
a small, terrible, self-mounted trophy.

What to do? push it back
into the darkness behind the wall,
out of sight, out of mind,
or risk tearing its head off
by pulling it out into the light of day?
I was stuck, and let it be.

But each time I mount to that room
we meet, head to head.
It's exchanging feathers for bone,
a homely instance of—what?
futility? death and transfiguration?

Just one thing to do-
burn the barn down.

II

Junked by the jolly carpenter,
tossed out the barn-office window,
along with shards of sheetrock,
worn-out shingles, ripped-out planks,
it lies rigid as the board beside it,
silent beak calling for last rites.
A quick little burial perhaps?
Cross of twigs? Pillar of pine-cone?

Not quick enough
It's easier to pop the bird
into a black plastic bag along
with the other stuff—
burned on the town dump,
it will return to air
in pure, featherless flight.

Is that just garbage?
I carry the bag to the road.

COULDN'T WAIT

yarmulke (Yiddish): skullcap

After tearing back in from the deck ttonight,
as is her wont, Cat Kassie, strangely,
makes herself scarce. Later, going up
to bed, I find out why. Deposited
on the carpet is a bird , deeply dead,
smuggled past my sight
in the cat's earlier rush. The corpse,
beautiful, looks damp, its absolute
stillness the antithesis of birdy
jitteriness. Spotted generously
with white, it is, appropriately,
dressed mostly in black. Not a real birder,
I make it out to be a downy woodpecker,
though lacking the standard
red micro-yarmulke assigned to it
by the guidebook. Have I discovered
a variant, should I put in a claim
to such, have it named after me,
one-time yeshivah boy who long ago
discarded his own yarmulke?

Just kidding. The real question is: what
was the bird doing out so late?
Whoever heard of a woodpecker
doubling as a night owl? What aberration
drove it from sleep and safety into Kassie's claws?
Couldn't it have waited for death
to be duly delivered by daylight?

NATURE ON PBS

A cold-blooded reptile? Not on your life.
This baby marine iguana being pecked to death
by the handsome Galapagos hawk possessed
of two fierce, yellow, hell-minted coins
that pass for eyes, this baby iguana, I say,
exudes a blood as bright and warmly red
as any you or I would muster
under similar circumstances.

Thus comes to an end the baby's brilliant,
frantic, pause-punctuated, broken-field run
toward the safety of the sea, after dragging
itself up the inside of a 5,000-foot crater,
then scampering down the outside,
the same inside and outside its mother
had traversed in reverse when seeking
a safe place to lay her eggs after her mate of a minute,
dragging her by the neck, had had his way with her.

The life force is imperious. It seizes the father-to-be
in its talons and drives him, it seizes the mother-to-be
in its talons and drives her, it seizes the new baby and drives it
into the talons of the hawk that will tear it to
pieces, delivering the chunks of fresh meat
to the two fluffy chicks in the nest,
with the bigger one always being fed first.

A HEATH FOR LEAR, A CORRIDOR FOR US

King Lear required a storm upon a heath
to bring him down from his crazy height,
acknowledge his, our, "bare forked animal."
Another sort of fall may await any of us,
a plunge into a hospital, our robe a thin,
back-split gown, our scepter the I-V stand
we clutch as we traverse our kingdom,
the corridor, glancing into its many rooms,
wondering what breakdown of bone or blood,
of heart or gut, has brought the occupants there,
our intransigent bodies clawing back
the gift of themselves.

SAINTS
Saint Sebastian is typically portrayed as shot full of arrows

Sebastian, converted to a reverse porcupine,
Thomas à Becket, struck dead by swords,
Joan of Arc transformed to a torch,
Agnes of Rome, age 13, fatally knifed in the throat,
Ignatius of Antioch, fed to lions in the Colosseum....
The list goes on and on, of bodies sacrificed
to belief, eyes fixed on the next world.

This world seems unlikely to give us
fresh instances of such martyrdom,
but shift the frame of reference and saints
are still among us, as with this mother
in the supermarket, steadily pushing
her wheelchaired son down the aisle,
his legs in braces, the boy unable
to hold his head up, to speak clearly,
victim of some genetic catastrophe.

For the mother, there will be no dark glamour
of a swift, terrible death, no canonization,
only being stretched on the rack of each day,
only having to open her eyes each morning
on the child that can never grow up,
never walk, never relinquish its necessary,
terrible grip on her, never stop pushing
her loving attentiveness to its limits.

SLICES OF LIFE

I

Released for the moment from imprisoning incisors,
the field mouse is allowed a few convulsions
before being taken up again by the cat
who lost a leg last year to a speeding car.

II

On a Pacific island, a soldier
not quite dead had his cheeks sliced open
by a G.I. intent on knocking out
the Jap's gold teeth.

III

Veterinarians have determined
that close to half of Canadian baby seals,
clubbed or shot annually to be turned into coats,
are still conscious when skinned.

V

One could continue but never get to the end,
never catch all the instances along the way,
the whole tapestry of pain unrolling from the Fall
till now, embedded, acceptable, in God's eyes only.

ARGUMENT BY DESIGN

Coming down this morning, geared, as always,
to feed the cat first, I find that Honey Boy,
named both for coat and disposition,
has set out, on the dining room floor,
his own breakfast array,
four dark, red gobbets, giving no clue
as to the living creature they were torn from—
mouse? vole? bird? flying squirrel?

Trying to recover the norm, I put on the radio,
tuned, as always, to NPR, and hear of an epidemic
of rape in Liberia, some of the victims tiny babies.

I want to haul an argument-by-design advocate
before the Cosmic Court of Justice, and press him
to say what we might infer about the Creator
from these components of His Creation, hoping
he will not slip the noose by contending
that there is a parallel universe to this one,
that ours is simply the great bin of God's rejects.

ON THE ESTATE FARM

Walking a trail, I see random clusters of them,
the few calves either grazing like veterans,
or else determinedly attached to their mothers'
teats, the adults in tree-shade, motionless, silent,
so much bulk with so little will to impose,
a beautiful lack of intention in their big black eyes,
a perfect fit of bovine bodies and being-ness.

A noise in the distance draws my attention—
at the far end of a field, I see
a single file of cows moving at a steady pace,
not trotting, and nobody in sight
either leading or goading them,
yet seemingly caught up in a forced march—
they are sending forth a cacophony of moos,
bellows, blaws , sounds beyond our vocabulary,
cries of creatures at the mercy of some human purpose—
are they all being led to slaughter, to serve
the estate's celebrated four-star restaurant?

Should you know, please keep it to yourself.

CHRISTMAS EVE AT THE UNITARIAN CHURCH

Claiming to know the truth kills the spirit,
proclaims the minister. Continually asking
questions is the only answer, he says, and,
more than that, we must love the questions.

Leaving, still aglow from the ceremony
which ended with each congregant
holding a candle lit by another's
in the darkened sanctuary, we get
into our car, turn out of the driveway,
and within a hundred yards spot
some sort of little corpse in the middle
of the road. A fresh kill—it hadn't
been there two hours earlier. A few feet
away lies its tail, as if a separate entity.
I curse, and you begin to rail against
careless drivers. Fury, fury, fills the car.

I'll try to love the questions. Yet
these facts, these dark facts in the headlights
that drive the questions, what
am I supposed to do with them?.
And am I to love what I've just asked?

THE SUFFERING PLANET

Clapped into a glass jar, cap screwed on,
this little bug is headed for the extension service
to determine whether or not it is a termite.
One of its wings obscurely injured, it can
only crawl, and I wonder if it is suffering,
wonder whether it will have been asphyxiated
by the time of its arrival.

Do bugs require oxygen? Can they suffer?
The ants I trained sunbeams on, as a boy
experimenting with his magnifying glass,
certainly gave a good imitation of it,
writhing as they crinkled into shriveled corpses.

Did the wriggling worms I threaded onto hooks
to catch brook trout experience anything
like we would if similarly impaled?
What of the lobsters I toss into boiling pots,
who exchange their subdued greenish-brown
for ostentatious orange-red as they cook to death?

There was no question of the suffering, however
brief, endured by the kitten I inadvertently scared
out of its hiding place, driving it into the path
of a car, where, struck, it convulsed its life away,
blood spurting from its mouth.

Mengele deliberately fractured a boy's skull,
waited for it to heal, then fractured it once more,
repeating the procedure tiil the boy could hardly
stagger toward the doctor, and died.

No Mengeles, we still leave a trail
of suffering behind us, our implication in it
sometimes out of view, as when we take drugs
or undergo procedures for what ails us,
after these have first been tested on
lab animals, mutilated, infected,
operated on, having been permanently
sequestered from an ordinary life
in nature, though that life is hardly a refuge from pain,
as with the lioness attacked by males,
her back broken, taking two days to die.

O, great Chain of Being,
great Chain of Suffering.

OUTSIDE THE GATES OF EDEN

Eden may be gone, but not the paradisal,
as with this nursery run by a husband and wife,
set amid flowing hills of the western Catskills,
holding, in addition to the mostly usual flora,
a dozen cats, who move easily among the visitors,
romping in spurts, rolling, dabbing
at each other, each named by the owners,
not one slated for a killing shelter.

At a distance stands a horse, rescued
from the slaughter-house, along with
two dozen sheep whose marvelously thick,
long coats, the wife tells us, cannot
always find a buyer, but who are maintained,
nevertheless, in this domain of luxuriant vistas,
humans and animals seamlessly joined,
an arrangement transcending God's garden,
where man has "dominion" over all creatures.

If the Old Testament comes to mind here
(if only by way of contrast), so does the New,
through the nursery's Passion vines,
whose flowers' components, the wife tells us,
have been taken to represent, one by one,
the lance that pierced Christ, the whips
that scourged Him, His five wounds,
the three nails that held Him stapled to the Cross—
thus, suffering is acknowledged even in this refuge.

The bumper sticker on the owners' car reads
"Smile—God Loves You." Should this evoke
the scorn of one of my own kind, the fallen
from faith, I would turn and say,
"This place has earned those words—
look to the place you usually stand in,
and bless this one."

BUYING A LITTLE MORE TIME

After parking my car, I notice,
lying in the road, beside a maroon
puddle, a squirrel on its side,
intact, though undeniably dead.
I walk toward the market,
but unable to stand the image
of the squirrel's inevitable squashing,
turn back, arm myself with a tissue, gingerly
pick up the corpse by its tail,
and place it in the planting area beside the store,.
the earth there seeming kinder
than the macadam where it met its end.

Of course crows will find it, or maggots,
or whatever finally dissolves any of our flesh,
but I needed to buy its body a little more time,
the gray fur, the adept paws, the once undulating tail.

AT THE DAY-CARE CENTER

Shane, 4, of the long, auburn
hair many women would kill for,

has a rickety walk that threatens,
with each step, to topple her,
is intimidated by a big-screen video game
the other kids are relishing.

Her story? She suffered a stroke
in the womb. I'll say that again:
she suffered a stroke in the womb.

Was it a case of Intelligent Design
caught napping? Or should we fall
back on the default position of God
moving in mysterious ways
His wonders to perform?

Now I'm having a game of catch with her
on the playground, using a large, soft ball,
trying to make the short tosses as easy
as possible for her to handle.
I'm doing the same as I do
with the other kids, and, as with
the other kids, she's having trouble
not flinching, trouble keeping her eye
on the ball, dropping it more often
than not. Careful as I try to be,
one toss hits her in the face. She giggles.
Another toss does the same
and she giggles again. I say:
your nose is trying to catch
the ball. More giggles.

For a few minutes, I like to think,
a kind of womb has been created here,
featuring a small heroine.

TIME: 6:45 A.M. PLACE: HEAVEN

Having taken a piss, I return to bed,
hoping against hope to go back to sleep.
In floats the new kitty, still unnamed,
though watching her drift from room to room
I've thought of her as "Little Cloud,"
impelled by some mysterious wind.

Till now, she's had only a series of failures
to show for her efforts, but this time,
determinedly clawing her way up,
she scales the high antique bed. Celebrating,
her little throat-motor at full throttle,
she ceaselessly traverses her new domain,
up and down, across and back,
writhings and undulations aided
and abetted by my ceaseless caresses,
rewarded in their turn by sandpaper tongueings.
Time melts away, space contracts to this bed.

Touch (presumably unavailable to the angels)
has here reached its apogee, in this union
of hand and fur, of human and animal,
in this marriage made here, here,
as I've noted above, in heaven.

MY HIPPO

It was love at first sight .

On a shelf at the back
of the African imports store,
reclining, but with her turned head
showing alertness, a hippo
from Zimbabwe, carved
from mottled, greenish shenstone,
drew me helplessly to her,
made me marvel at the great, pop-eyed head,
compelled me to stroke and lift her,
shocking me with her sheer weight.

But why was I surprised?
Isn't the hippo the ultimate fatty,
impatiently repudiating any thoughts
about the unbearable lightness of being?
So frank about her bulk, she asures us
she will do her best to keep that enormous
snout filled with hippo goodies,
maintain the fleshy folds behind her head,
glory in her suave rotundity,
her small ears offering little passageway
to any propaganda emanating
from Weight Watchers of the Wild.

"BLESSED ARE THE MEEK FOR THEY SHALL INHERIT THE EARTH"

It's safe to say Jesus got that wrong.
More likely, it will be Exxon Mobil or its ilk,
though in the long run the lucky legatees
may be cockroaches or bacteria or viruses.

If I could choose, I'd leave the water planet
to Canada geese. I know, I know,
they've become a nuisance bird,
but only from our narrow perspective,
and is any species a greater nuisance
than our own? Consider the elegance
of the goose's elongated black neck,
its refusal when crossing a road
in the face of an oncoming car
or pedestrian to give up the dignity
of its deliberate stride. Consider, too,
its love of water, its mating for life,
its fierce protection of its goslings.

Beauty, courage, an appreciation
of what makes earth unique, a sense
of family values—placed beside these,
all that poop pales.

WHAT WONDERFUL LIFE?
Camp Sandyville,
Summer 1942

for Frank Capra

Doing the crawl at the deep end of the plank crib,
without ever having learned proper breathing,
I am beginning to gasp and flail. A counselor
missing nothing reaches down, grasps me
by the elbows, pulls me straight up
as any breaching whale into the blessed air.

It is my second brush with death, the first
having come when a car halted only a foot
away from me as I blithely, manically zigzagged
across the gutter in a game of hopscotch.
Later, my mother was told that the screeching
brakes could be heard two blocks away.

Beside putting a hole in her heart, what difference
would my early exit from this world have made?
No George Bailey, mine has not been a wonderful life—
I have not rescued a younger brother from death,
prevented a druggist from botching a prescription,
saved a lovely woman from lonely spinsterhood,

stood between my townspeople and a grasping banker.
It may be unfair to measure my stay here
or anybody's stay by the movies, but who
can remove those images from our heads,
who take us firmly by the arm, counsel
and console us as we exit from the theater
into the air of the ordinary?

ZEYDE
zeyde: (Yiddish): grandfather

Small, bent, wizened, hidden
behind whiskers,Yiddish, tobacco fumes,
and the Talmud, my grandfather sat alone
in his kitchen, an exile,
while my grandmother queened it
in the living room.
Had he really once mounted her, and repeatedly,
to produce my aunts, my uncles, my mother?
Was I actually connected to him?

Only decades later did I take in
the casual heroism that had enabled him
to pull up out of the Hungarian known,
sell store and mill, gather wife
and eight children for the odyssey to America
(losing and burying the baby en route).

What have I ever done to set beside that?

THEOLOGY AT THIRTEEN

Which would be the preferable sin, I agonized,
as I rushed from my new, secular high school
into the impending Sabbath darkness
of a frigid midwinter Friday?
To transgress at length the prohibition
against labor, by walking the long way home
carrying my considerable load of books,
or, to shorten, perhaps dilute, wrongdoing,
but only by daring to board a forbidden bus,
transportation also barred once the light had failed ?

Precisely because walking would be harder,
even painful, the punishment being meted out
in exact alignment with the commission of the sin,
(a scheme Dante couldn't have improved on),
that's what I chose, that's what I deserved,
for having been, recent yeshivah boy,
too timid to ask the authorities for a change
of program that would have allowed me
to leave school early so as to observe the Sabbath..

Better yet, walking would guarantee
my arriving home too late to attend
even a part of Friday night service, more
cause for guilt, more sure punishment
in store for the Prodigal Son.
Wasn't Father going to be proved right
for having opposed my breaking away
from parochial school, my insisting
on going to godless Samuel J. Tilden?

When, after an experience of eternity,
I arrived home, I found Father,
returned from synagogue, setting the table,
a domestic gesture rare for him (my mother
having allowed herself a pre-dinner nap).
That quiet man, seeing me, said nothing,
but, raising his fistful of forks on high,
brought them sharply down, their clattering crash
against the board piercing my skull,
a fragment that has proved inoperable.

JOE HOLDER BLOWS THE SHOFAR

For my young self, the shofar's meanings
were a blank—I knew only that the thing
had to be sounded as part of the celebration
of the Jewish New Year, and that it was *my* father—
o, cursed fate!—who was the designated blower.

Brought to center stage at the synagogue,
this usually quiet man was expected to produce
a host of shaped sounds—*tekiah, shevorim, teruah*—
relentlessly called for by the cantor.
At least, that was the theory of the thing,
and when my father managed to bring it off,
I was relieved, in fact, proud. But the shofar
was a hell of a horn to play, and at times
my father's breath gave out (what did he expect,
he who had begun smoking at the age of eight?),
and I shrank into my shame. Small consolation
that the second-string blower held the shofar
upside down (absurd!) and could not
match my father's timbre.

Hours after the service, with the house quiet
and my parents napping, I would gingerly
remove the shofar from its case in the dining room,
note its smoothness, its striated coloring
and scalloped tip, put it to my lips, take in the taste
of tobacco, and blow as hard as I could.. All I ever got
were pathetic sputterings, or absurd farting sounds.

I don't remember ever telling my father of these failed
attempts. They probably sank into the ongoing silence
between us. But for better or worse , I was never more
his son than when he raised the shofar to his lips.

BROOKLYN EPIPHANY
Summer 1943

Once upon a time, in Crown heights,
there appeared a sky, so leaden, so low,
it seemed as if it might crush the rooftops,
continue descending, and smother
the very street where, daily, at age ten,
I ran free with my friends.

Coming up to bat midway through
a stickball game, unable to get out
from under that sky, I fell
into a sudden depression, my interest
in the contest snuffed out. Mumbling
something or other to my team-mates,
I surrendered the broom-handle, walked away.
I had to get upstairs, had to climb
to our apartment, where my mother would be.

No lights turned on, the only illumination
coming through the kitchen window,
she stood with her back to it, ironing,
her face barely lit, her head and torso
framed by that very sky.

I stood there, unable to say anything,
taking pity on how hard she worked,
seeing her as lonely, knowing now
that someday she would die.

OCTOBER FALLS

I

Red, yellow, orange,
trees have turned theatrical,
unsustainably brilliant,
leaves, on fire, falling
and shriveling to crinkled corpses.

II

This morning I fell on the tennis court,
blood spurting from my cheek,
bright as any falling leaf.

III

There was nothing brilliant
about my mother's October
fall from the top of her front steps,
the first and only plunge
of her careful life.

No leaf, she fell as any object
would, stroke-struck perhaps,
her only colors the blue-black
of the bruise above her left eye,
and, one day later, dead,
the pallor of her bloated face.

WILD ROSES

Mind moves in mysterious ways.
How else explain this memory, erupting
as I drive to the bank to refinance
my Connecticut home yet again,
this memory of wild roses that grew
behind the house my parents rented,
in Brooklyn's un-wild Crown Heights?

The roses climbed the ramshackle trellis separating
our microscopic, concrete-bound backyard
from our neighbor's, and when the trellis fell
they kept on growing.

I never paid them much attention back then,
their mere smudges of pink and white,
poor relations, after all, of *real* roses,
those aristocrats with their petals
elegantly gathered in tight concentric cups.

And come October, the wild roses were put to shame
by the pair of euonymus which pretty much filled the yard.
Nondescript during the summer,
these did a slow turn to stunning purple,
two burning bushes side by side,
igniting the surrounding air.

But now it is the spunky, proletarian wild roses
that rise in, that fill, the garden of remembrance.
The tears rise, the road blurs—here's the bank.

AT THE FUNERAL

The box up front doesn't matter.
My Uncle Jay is certainly elsewhere,
though don't ask me for the exact location.

A troupe of clowns, some chalked,
some rouged, has taken over the chapel.
What else can I call these mourners,
purporting to be my relatives?
"Uncle Mark" stands there, ruddy, cute,
as wordless as ever, but twice his age.
My "aunts," dark-haired beauties in real life,
have shown up as shrunken blondes.
And is that Morty, first-born cousin,
always on, joking, ready to break into his tenor?
Why is he hiding inside that person at the end
of the next pew, pasty-faced, abstracted, silent?
Could this be cousin Judy, adventuress of bars,
whose perfect skin simmered even as she struggled
to get a complete sentence out?
Her stand-in, pale, dumpy, turns in slow motion,
and murmurs something appropriate.

No matter. After the show, the eulogies,
the trip to the cemetery, the burial,
they'll all disperse, and I'll find the originals ,
young, brilliant, in the old family album,
and in home movies, shown at odd times,
within my skull.

AT TWILIGHT

...casual flocks of pigeons make
Ambiguous undulations as they sink,
Downward to darkness, on extended wings.
    —Wallace Stevens

Mid-March moth, come from God knows where,
you struggle up the window-pane,
pulled to the light that is dying
as surely as you are.
Your wings draw closed, then flatten out,
as you spasm, flop, and resume
your upward crawl to nowhere.

Soon it is over.
More modest than Stevens's pigeons ,
you have folded your wings,
and remain, a jagged sail upon the sill,
your own monument to your small struggle.
I swear never to sweep you away.

Wait a minute. You're not dead.
You're at it *again,* climbing and foundering.
Get out of my poem.

REMEMBERING SPRING

Another bitch of a March day,
sky suddenly going gray, contemptuously
flinging down a salting of snow,
then turning the sun back on
but only to mock us, as the wind
probes our cheekbones with a cold scalpel.

The ground, impastoed with dead leaves,
flecked by muddy pools, the trees reduced
to bare essentials, we need more
than Daylight Savings Time to save us.

We must strain to remember the something
underground somehow in touch
with light and air, the powerful creature
that will come into view disguised as the delicate—
the leaf, the blossom, the spear of grass.

CROCUSES

Smashing the speed records of weeds,
these open their bright beaks overnight,
content to live on cold air, cold water.

Scouting the start of Spring,
they are scalped by the Indian-giver,
who puts them so early to bed,
for being so early to rise.

PERFECTION

Mocked for the whole
of my suburban sojourn

by Scott's picture-perfect lawns
gleaming their Platonic green

at me from magazines and screen,
I welcome this stretch of rainforest

spring, the waters coming down and down
and down again, transforming

my hitherto miserable yard
into a set fit for a lawn-food shoot.

Mowing this new fullness, I tread
a continuum of coifed greens

flowing from country clubs
and great estates. But hold on—

just ahead of me appears a stand
of six buttercups, consorting

with a motley crew of other
nervy aliens. Driven by

the perfect-lawn imperative,
I am about to mow them all down,

when Frost's "A Tuft of Flowers"
comes to mind. Of course mine

has not been spared by some prior
mower, but the seed of swerving

has been planted by that poem,
so that now an upstart islet

floats on a green lake.

TO SWAT OR NOT TO SWAT

"Bang, you're dead, first fly of spring"—
that's what I might have said just before
my swatter thwacked the clear-winged creature
clinging to a window screen this morning
as if frozen there. It fell to the counter,
where it lay on its back, not quite dead,
as a matter of fact, but quivering.

So cold-blooded just a moment before,
I felt a surge of mercy, picked it up
in a tissue and gently squeezed
the remaining life out of it.
Another day, another small death.

But is there such a thing?
If, as we have been told, a butterfly
fanning its wings in Mexico
can produce a storm thousands of miles away,
who knows what my little act of murder
may bring forth, if not right away?

Will some attendant chain of consequences
take down the Golden Gate Bridge,
or poison all the clams in Chesapeake Bay?
Will a cancer epidemic envelop Chicago,
or has an asteroid started to head for New York?

I wouldn't bet on it. But maybe some other chain
has begun unfolding, a small one,
somewhere in my cortex,
so that somewhere down the line,
not even remembering the fly,
I'll refrain from swatting someone,
withholding my hand, biting my tongue.

AFLAME IN SPRING

Another screw-up by Verizon,
by Chase, Toyota, Microsoft, Staples,
another aria of irritation emanating from me,
as, ranting on the phone, I roam
through this still unsettled apartment,
victim once more of the world's refusal
to work well, of the perpetrators'
withdrawal behind a regress of *menus*
designed only to starve us, as we dangle
below the telephone holds from hell.

Was I born to spend my days
this way, in spleen-soaked sputtering?

Perhaps so. Consider our beautifully rounded
source of life, coming into His own
these days with Daylight Savings Time.
Is He not, at His calmest, always aboil,
spouting flares and coronal mass ejections,
to say nothing of His continual hydrogen hissy fits?

The apple does not fall far from the tree.
Can this son fall far from his Father?

HERDING LEAVES

The last round-up for these critters,
you could say—thousands of them
mixed in with hundreds of acorns,
death and potential new life
all scrambled together in fall's motley,
the whole kit and caboodle fleeing, panicked,
in the face of the directed whirlwind kicked up
by my bright-red leaf-blower, artfully cutting
off their retreat, driving them into cowed piles,
to be raked onto a tarp, dragged off to the entropy
of the nearby woods, which have seen all this before.

REPLACEMENTS WANTED

These angels are headed for the garage
to take thetr winter snooze.
Of course they're not real ones—airy, fluid, alert,
gadding about on God-appointed rounds—
no, not these concrete-cast demos of gravity,
purchased at the garden-supply store.
Nesting all summer long in dead-nettle ground cover,
eyes, wings supposedly guarding the garden,
they kept less than perfect watch.

Right under their angelic noses
disdainful deer munched on the day-lilies,
while who-knows-what dug up the mulch.
Not Heaven, but stinky Bobex, finally came to the rescue.
Still, who can fault these sweet air-heads,
daydreaming through summer days,
in serene remove from garden labors,
mosquito bites, embedded ticks?
As cold and its consequences come clamping down,
who shall serve as their replacements?

SLEEPERS

Wrapped in nothing less than mystery,
profoundly alone in doing what they share
with everyone, dead to the world
but connected helter-skelter to it,
sleepers, whatever their pasts,
are innocent as eggplants, profoundly
neutral, their only imprint on the world
their exhales, and who can begrudge them those?

Not one jot of history has been committed
by a sleeper, not one plot or betrayal,
not one unforgivable stupidity or
unthinkable cruelty—they have all
floated free of action, even if,
in their sealed-off brains, they are
being lashed by wish or disappointment,
goaded by fear or rage, imagining
the unthinkable or simply the incoherent.

Let sleepers lie—some secret business
of the universe might be at work
in their stillness, and even if not,
isn't each a thing of wonder?

AER LINGUS, FLIGHT 111

Grateful to have been vaulted
over the wide waters and not
plunged into the profound Atlantic,
to have felt only low-grade terror
during the stretches of turbulence,
to have been brought back down to earth
with just the slightest of bumps.

As we join in the spontaneous applause
of our fellow passengers, are we simply
acknowledging the skill of our never-seen
pilot, who has held us all in the palm of his hand,
or are we concealing, by a kind of ironic humor,
relief at having survived yet another
scheduled miracle, a numbered transatlantic flight?

The short-lived community of the flown-together
begins to break up, with the pulling down of bags,
the antsy wait for the aisle's log-jam to clear,
the endless walk to the luggage conveyor,
the tense tedium of watching for our suitcases
to appear, then, with awkward lungings,
the bringing to a halt their sedate little joyride.

Fellow passengers now left completely behind,
we get into our hired car, and enter
the Great American Centrifuge.

Even at thirty thousand feet
there had been no escape from the human prosaic—
the matter-of-fact eating, viewing, chatting, snoozing.
Only down here, looking up
from the clogged spoke of the Long Island Expressway,
do the planes, taking off, assume
their severe abstraction, their ascent
as silvery, self-propelled arrows.

BETWEEN THE ASPHALT AND THE BLUE SKY

Who could have seen this coming?
Here I am, listening to Prairie Home Companion's
annual joke show, jokes coming at you rat-a-tat-tat,
some being told by a Scottish musician,
who says his next piece is called "Sarah's Song."
I'm expecting a jaunty, bouncy, jiggy ditty
and instead, here comes this pure instrumental,
played on, for God's sake an accordion,
usually my least favorite instrument,
but I find my heart being squeezed, squeezed ,
mugged –the joking had set me up—
by the Celtic genius for melancholy,
and tears are running down my face
as I sit here in my parked car, in front of CVS ,
between the asphalt and the blue sky.

What am I to Sarah or Sarah to me
that I should weep for her? What
is she so sad about, anyway?
And why isn't her song being *sung*?
But more than anything else,
how does such music do what it does to us?
Is there some great aquifer of tears
underlying the entire globe,
and do some strings of notes
simply dig an instant well down into it,
releasing its waters upward
through some invisible piping we all carry
within us , suddenly making us cry
no matter what we are doing,
as we go about our horizontal business,
here, between the asphalt and the blue sky?

SUN, LAKE, PIZZA BOX

A quarrel at breakfast, then, angry silence.

Trying to redeem at least a part of the day,
we take a drive into the crystal, November afternoon,
stopping at a lake we've always just whizzed past.
A small sign gives its name, which I keep repeating,
taking pleasure in its exotic syllables.

We gaze and gaze as a slight wind sends an infinite series
of lulling ripples across the lake surface, directly
away from the low-hung sun, which has made
a segment of the view stressful—
try to look at it straight on and you're being
blinded by a fierce god who withholds
seeing even as he floodlights the scene, withholds
warming even as he supplies the planet's
essential heat. Wanting contact, but anticipating
a cold reception, I cautiously dip my fingers
into the light-fragmenting water. It's warmer
than expected. Before we leave, we embrace.

Here, perhaps, on this Sunday drive,
we have touched, in the soothing, mothering water,
in the ferociously fathering, implacable sun,
one more set of the governing poles of our world,
their force fields making for the middlingness
of our lives, the human muddle, the mishmash
of anger and love, meanness and tenderness,
the capacity for thoughtless littering, as with
that empty pizza box lying at the water's edge,
and for reverent naming. as with Lake Lillinonah,
Lake Lillinonah.

AT STOP & SHOP

As if towed by an invisible line,
the tiny girl follows directly
in her burly father's wake, as he plunges
into the produce section of the mega-market,
his broad back fully turned on her.
How could that bull have sired
this child made of china? How could
he allow her to be so obliterated
by lettuce, tomatoes, stringbeans, whatever?
I, childless, just stand there,
wishing the girl were mine. Then her feet
would never touch the floor, she would be
carried and kissed continually as we moved
amid the zucchini, artichokes, broccoli rabe,
Swiss chard, arrugula, father and daughter
at Stop & Shop, larking in an unfallen garden.

A VISIT BY CAILIN, AGE TWO-AND-A-HALF

Whence comes this sorcery,
enchanted, enchanting child?
Does it derive from your mix of genes,
Scotch-Irish, Italian, Jewish, Episcopalian?
Probably not, in an America
so generally mixed up to begin with.
No, the mystery of your power
endures, as you ascend effortlessly
to the throne from which you reign
over a court of adoring adults,
stunned into total fidelity
by the joy of gazing on you.

Yes, you have turned us all
into Johnny-come-lately monarchists.
Vying to be appointed your jester,
my forty-something son-in-law hops
around the house, transformed
into a giant goony bird, a playmate
you chase after, giggling.
Great-aunt Barbara, would-be lady in waiting,
wonders how to inveigle an invitation
to your new palace in New Jersey.
Desiring to be your Raleigh,
I, Great-uncle Alan, silently wish
that you would ask for the moon,
so I could begin at once my expedition
to plant your flag there.

But none of us can compete for your favor
with the cat (self-exiled to the master bedroom).
Determined to knight her, you toil
up the long staircase majestically,
undeterred by the unmistakable load
in your diaper, an olfactory fact
you so regally ignore.

Ruling over language as easily as you rule over us,
you repeatedly utter "huh," not
as a question, but a statement,
and who dares challenge the Queen's English?

To hell with "My country 'tis of thee"—
we sing "God Save Our Gracious Queen,"
Cailin the Incandescent.

MRI R.I.P.

Stupidly assuming it would be of the open
variety, I find myself, prone, being shoved
into an enclosed MRI machine, told
the exam will take about 25 minutes,
and given a little rubber bulb to squeeze
if I need the attendant. Claustrophobe that I am,
I feel deeply betrayed, disbelieving
how close to my face is the top
of the cylinder. Here is a form of burial
alive, my absolutely favorite nightmare.

In what I take as one of my greatest lifetime
achievements, I neither scream, nor shriek,
nor curse, nor spastically squeeze the bulb,
nor attempt to claw myself out of the infernal
device, but, rather, count seconds, convert
them to minutes. and so stick it out without even—
as would be normal for me—breaking into a sweat.

But I cannot break out of the aftermath
of that encasement: thinking about the time
when I shall be buried for real, my face just
inches below the coffin lid, my brain retaining—
this is irrational, I know, but I can't let go
of the possibility—my brain retaining
a shred of consciousness.

If I had my druthers, if I could make up the rules
and rites of life and death , this is how it would be:
a corpse would be carried up, up
to a mountain top, laid out unburied,
all of its parts defunct, except for its eyes
and the portion of its brain that registers sight,
and so, night and day, take in, for all of time to come

sky's light, sky's dark, sun, stars, the plumping
and thinning of the moon, and, above all,
in their varying degrees of luminosity,
the drifting, ever-shifting free spirits of the clouds.

10 DRUMMER LANE
REDDING CT.

for Igor Kipnis

The house was on the market for years.
Before its being taken off, the owner
was himself taken. But the name remains
on the mailbox. I note it with pleasure,
each time I walk past, always hearing,
in my mind's ear, the plucked, tinny
tinklings of his much recorded harpsichord.

The only keyboard I can play is this computer's,
and I play it now, hoping, in its clacking,
to pay what tribute I can to him, who filled
the world's ears with the cascadings of Scarlatti,
the ingenuities of Bach. Oh, let the name remain
where it is, a small, still point—Kipnis—
in the turning, turning, tuning of the world.

ON SEEING A PHOTO OF
BROWNIE TROOP 745
in *The Redding Pilot*

No matter how close up we hold
the faces in old photos, how hard
we gaze at them, their owners stay
stubbornly embalmed in silver nitrate,
immune to the questions we would put to them.

Now consider this photo from last week's paper,
as gripping as if shot by Matthew Brady,
though obviously no question here of faces
sealed away under the glaze of the past—
rather, each of these caught countenances
seems to beacon its owner's future.

Placed at the apex of the group
(the photographer knew what he was doing),
is the pack's indubitable queen,
not the prettiest of the girls,
but self-crowned by way of her aura.
This is *her* domain, and she shall reign
wherever she goes—posing now
is simply practice, an early photo op.

Arranged beneath her are her subjects.
One girl's poised and humorous expression
says she will sail through whatever comes her way,
while the variety of unease displayed by others
foretells a confinement to dog-paddling
in the sea of upcoming circumstances.

Not so with the group's beauty, stationed
in the row just below the queen—lips
slightly parted, but not smiling, she is looking
off to her right. Is she simply daydreaming,
or has she been stunned by what she intuits
of the Troy in which she may find herself?

Bookending her row are two disturbing girls.
The one on the left looks determinedly down,
so she has not miscalculated by a millisecond
before the shutter snap, but has chosen
to remain immersed in her depression—she is not
of this domain, nor may she ever join another.

Her counterpart on the right, not quite contained
by the frame, seems to have wandered into the picture
from some arena of unspeakable suffering—
right hand partly covering her face, a finger
to her lips, her large eyes, bearing dark circles,
look not at, but through, the camera.
It appears that she has seen and will continue to see
things undreamt of in Redding,
named five years running as
"Best little own in Connecticut."

ON THE TRAIN

Descended from a pre-Raphaelite painting,
the young blonde, seated aslant on the aisle,
never takes her gaze from her boyfriend,
offering the rest of us only her profile,
her long curls mingling with a dangling earring.

Six feet away, ensconced in a wheelchair,
sits a woman of similar age, sallow,
adorned only by a barrette, head helplessly
bobbing and weaving as she speaks gutturally
to her elderly female companion.

Neither young woman can view the other.
It's just as well.
Why should the first have her perfection
roiled by seeing the second, already
deep in her doom? Why should the second,
pierced by some errant DNA, have to look
on the bared, perfect teeth of unfairness?

The train rushes on, delivering us all
to the rest of our lives.

ON OUR WAY

Some die promenading the decks,
some in their cabins.
Some are flung overboard,
a few leap.
Some fall beside the engines,
pistons gone still.

Laughter floats across the water
from the ship behind us,
thronged with the oblivious young.

Shrouded more each day,
the ship ahead makes do
with a skeleton crew.

In just a matter of years,
we shall reach the brimming edge.

IN PRAISE OF CHARCOAL

The real stuff I mean, not those bagged things
looking like some machine's droppings,
but *charcoal,* its chips appearing to be
survivors of some global catastrophe,
yet, hefted, of unearthly lightness,
as if the weigher stood on moon's brightness.

Heated up in the hibachi, they sing,
that is, emit a distant tinkling,
so, burning, endear themselves to the ear
before turning to ashes and air.

Humble servants, cooks, lovely dark chimes,
tinkle a while longer in these rhymes.

ODE TO MY FEET

Oh, wondrous moving pedestals,
improbable supporters of my body-tower,
you with your thick-fringed fronts,
with your lovely oval backs,
with your subtly arced inner sides,
you wait, patient as mules,
while I stand in line, shave,
or, all too seldom, star-gaze,
yet are ready, with no prior notice,
to arch up, lift off and move forward,
in brilliant coordination.

You have lent yourselves to kicking
cans, stones, footballs or someone's ass
(if only in my imagination).
You do not complain about being sheathed
in shoes (though you show some
passive-aggressive smelliness there),
plainly loving going bare
over grass or beach sand.

Be with me always.
There is nothing lowly about you.

ON NOT STARING AT THE PACIFIC

For Richie and Marcia

Keats, famously, got it wrong when he perched
Cortez on that peak in Darien, but so, in a way,
did Balboa , who, facing eastward ,
called the calm sea he saw the "Pacific,"
which hardly covers all the facts. Nobody's perfect.

As for me, standing high above the beach at Point Reyes,
I can neither look down nor out for very long—
either way is frightening—space here seems able to kill
you or swallow you up in the glare of its wide expanse.

The baby cove near Carmel is what I can manage, its seals,
its close-by rocky prominence on which a gull has just taken
the place of two girls clambering down from the peak,
its sea otter, lolling on its back amid kelp,
presenting its whiskered white mug to any camera
that might be handy, the pretty touch of white water
continually churning at land's edge, the sea
content for now to do a finger exercise.

UP THE DRAIN

Goddamit, it's happened again—one careless
move on my part, though ever so miniscule,
and my left contact lens, paper-thin, transparent,
barely agreeing from the start to exist at all
in this fallen world, has itself fallen, slipped
from its tangential perch on my index finger into
my sink, but really the great sink, the universal catch-basin
of all lost things, never to be seen again,
especially by these myopic eyes.

Still, as usual, I do not surrender
without a struggle. Ritually fetching
a flashlight, I bend my near-blind gaze
to the sink's surface, visually scouring
every square inch for the elusive, rubbery wretch,
but meet only, as usual, glistening white porcelain
proclaiming its innocence: "Who, me? I never
seen no lens, mister, honest—you must be
thinking of another sink." "Really?" I say,
"I think you stink, you sink. I mean what
would it cost you to give up my lens?"

Nothing but white, wet silence. I am about
to fall into my usual fit of self-hatred
for having lost yet another thing, one more
item to be added to the lifelong-list
of my personal disappeared—
lead-heavy silver pen, blue leather clogs,
antique milk-bottle container, neurotically shy
first wife, etc. etc—when I decide
to transcend myself. No more
Mr. Surface, I am going to plumb
The Depths. Putting down my flashlight,

and steeling myself against the anticipated yuck,
I pull up sharply on the metal drainplug.

Yech—nothing but a long string of slimy
hair and whatever, dangling from the thing.
Now I must indeed concede defeat, admit
the lens to my aforementioned list of the utterly lost.

But wait—can it be? Soiled by its ordeal,
yet thereby made more visible, my lens rests
quietly in its disgusting nest, available even
to my failed vision, and in my joy I think:
Perhaps the accumulating crud of the world,
the gunk, the junk, the garbage, the discards,
the leavings, work, if only here and there,
and maybe only by chance, to redeem themselves,
to provide a soft landing, a refuge,
for the delicate and precious,
restoring at least some of what was thought lost.

I rinse the lens and place it in my eye—
ah, now I can see.

TOWARDS A TENNIS FRIEZE

The match is over. I walk off the court
after one more of my schizy efforts:
half a dozen brilliant shots, perhaps fifty
unforced errors. Doomed to repeatedly veer
away from form, I'm a loser, I'll never change,
not at this age. On the court adjoining,
a young girl— eight, nine—slender,
is taking a serving lesson from the pro.
Repeatedly, she tosses the ball way up, then freezes—
left arm vertically extended, head thrown way back,
trunk arched, inverted racket held behind her—
then releases, whipping the racket forward and
down. She's already good. Yet it's not her swing,
not tennis balls delivered to their target that hold me,
but that body delivered over each time to its stringent pose,
become a bow drawn taut, perfect servant of the serve,
fragment of a modern Parthenon, here,
frozen for a second, in this tennis bubble.

AT THE PHYSICAL THERAPIST

Muscle Chart

So this is us, or perhaps only guys—
tensed tissue, fibers abounding,
done up in blues and purples, running
the length of our bodies, names carrying
a Roman weightiness—trapezius, pectineus,
brachioradialus, sternocleidomastoid—
hands outspread in what could be seen
as a pleading gesture, but one belied
by the power radiating from the whole,
poised to step off the chart, crush
anything the world might care to offer.

Skeleton Chart

Who is this Tinkertoy pushover?
What stripped that glorious musculature
away? How does this assemblage
of bones manage to keep itself
upright? Femur and humerus
are particularly pathetic. And
what in the world does this creature
find to grin about? The pleading
hands here make sense—this loser
needs all the help he can get.

TUG OF WAR

> O death, where is thy victory,
> O grave, where is thy sting?
> —*Corinthians*

The contest begins the day you're born.
Unaware, you're automatically made an entrant.
It's always a one-sided affair,
devoid of a level playing ground.
In fact, there's no "level" at all.
The whole thing is on the vertical
and, at the start, apparently on the up and up.
You keep growing, up and up and up.
Before too long your cock stands up
or your nipples grow erect.
You rise in your profession.
You raise a family.
You raise your consciousness.

But then the other side gets down
to business. Time, it seem, has pull everywhere
and does not hesitate to use it,
as parents, friends, acquaintances, sometimes children,
are laid low. Gravity, there all the while
but a late bloomer, really kicks in.
Your flesh sags, your spirits droop.
you lose height, you're a downhill skier
out of control until the final tumble.
O grave, here is thy victory,
O death, you take the ring.

THE COSMOS INTRUDES
kvetch (Yiddish): complain

How does it happen that the Big Bang,
manifesting itself today, is succeeding
only in irritating me? Shouldn't it
always act as a spur to grand ruminations,
such as: Why has this orgasmic burst of creation,
its fruits ripening all over the universe,
also given us stars sickening and dying
everywhere, with who knows what other earthly
miseries showing up amid the galaxies?

But right now I don't have enough patience
to contemplate the Great Questions—I simply
want to kvetch about my latest brush with technology,
as I try to set up my new TV, carefully following
the instructions of techies who live in a universe
of their own, who fail to recognize the possibility
that when you flick your set on with the remote,
you may get nothing but snow and crackling,
embodiments, we are told, of background radiation
left over from the Big Bang, right here, right now,
in my bedroom—when all I wanted was HBO.

WHAT'S IT ALL ABOUT, UNIVERSE?

My left glove has managed to get itself lost
just minutes after the missing right one was found.
Left, right, lost, found—I guess there's
a certain symmetry here, but what interests me
is the cosmological constant of loss,
the fact that something is always going missing.

It can happen with people too.
My friend Tom died mysteriously at thirty-three.
Another friend, Ann, the picture of vigor,
went to sleep and never awakened.
My wife passed from discomfort
to death in less than an hour.
I mean, what's it all about, universe?
(Notice I 'm not addressing God here,
that hopeless Indian-giver—bless Him
for being that if you want to, but count me out.)

My question, simply put, is this: Why,
cosmos, do you labor for eons, stirring
stupendous stews of strings and supernovae,
generating a particular concatenation of atoms,
only to have it, him, her, abruptly disappear?

Is there something here I'm missing?

A VEGETARIAN WANNABE'S THEOLOGICAL RANT

shochet (Hebrew): ritual slaughterer
fleishing (Yiddish): of meat

"The fear of you and the dread of you shall be upon every beast
of the earth, and upon every bird of he air, upon everything that
creeps on the ground and all the fish of the sea; into your hand
they are delivered. Every moving thing that lives shall be food for
you...."
        —Genesis

That's quite an epigraph. Now, for some context.

Consider, though it might seem like a digression,
the Fall. Why didn't God allow those two
to taste of *anything* vegetative that grew in that blessed
place, forbidding them only whatever moved,
could look them in the eye, could vocalize
before ambling or trotting or galloping away?
Why didn't the Bible have Adam, in the face
of such a proscription, egged on by the Serpent
or not, pick up a stone, brain the nearest lamb, rip off
a piece of its flesh, eat it, raw or barbecued,
offering some to Eve, the two thus acquiring
the forbidden knowledge? Act and consequence
would then have been proportionately linked,
evil exemplified by sacrificing another creature
on the altar of one's appetite, and a mere fruit
not burdened with an impossible significance.

But God could not have scripted that scenario,
because He Himself would show a predilection
for flesh—remember how, later, He preferred
Abel's offering of the firstlings of his flock
to Cain's sacrifice of the fruits of the field –
so how could He possibly have blamed
Adam and Eve for sharing His taste?
And why did He come to command Noah
to have the animals walk two by two onto the Ark?
Not for pity of them, not to save them from the waters
for their own sakes, but because when they were allowed
to step back onto the newly dry land, it had to have been
as foreseen guarantors of meat, for when God
got a whiff of Noah's animal sacrifice after the Flood,
He was so pleased He made him the feared lord
and consumer of all other creatures (read the epigraph again).

To go back momentarily, to Eden—
some say nature fell when the first couple did,
the animals dividing only then into hunters and hunted.
But didn't that mean God thereby fell as well,
since only a profound withdrawal of empathy
could have let that happen?

Whatever the case, here is God's world as we find it:
Owls sinking their claws and beaks into soft,
panicked rabbits, skua birds seizing baby penguins,
snakes swallowing voles live and whole, hyenas
hounding and worrying wildebeests to death,
jaguars breaking the necks of gazelles,(gone
in an instant from astounding leapers to dangling
carrion), pigs and poultry stuffed into concentration camps,
veal calves, guilty of being born, imprisoned for all
of their short lives in straitjacket crates,
the slaughter-house worker firing bolt or bullet
into the skull of the bawling cow,
the shochet pulling back the head of the chicken
the better to slit its throat.

Christ might have dramatized the new order He wanted
by preaching abstention from everything *fleishig,*
but you could say He did better than that, in chasing
the sheep and oxen away along with the money-changers,
thereby disrupting the Temple practice of animal sacrifices,
soon becoming himself the Lamb of God, offered up
not on an altar but a cross, the last sacrifice
of flesh God would require—if you buy
that version of events.

But even if you do, consider this:
Hitler was a vegetarian.
And what about fish?

I'm working on it.

SUN WORSHIP

In the winter, in shockingly early late afternoon,
the sun, intent on leveling with you,
looks you in the eye, saying that in spite
of all appearances, it has been killing
itself to warm your little life,
that it is your dying, only god.

RETURN

noodge (Yiddish): pest
tumeler (Yiddish): a master of ceremonies who encourages guest or
audience participation

The sad business has come.

This cat who is too much for us, this in-your-face
nuzzler, this leap-onto-your-lap-so-he-can squirm-
        there bounder,
this against-your-leg butt-er, this Guinness Book of Records
feline-vertical-jump champ, this bare-limb
and-dining-room-table
engraver, this I-need-to-stick-my-face-into-anything-you-open-
especially-the-refrigerator, this noodge, this ten-pound tumeler,
this Ritalin-candidate kitty we named Kato
(think Pink Panther),
has got to be returned.

After a valiant struggle against my panicky thrusting
of him into the carrier, he proceeds to break
my heart with a show of strange restraint,
emitting just two little peeps of protest before settling in,
and almost falling asleep as I drive from Connecticut
into Westchester, cursing sluggish Route 6,
encountering one American nowhere after another,
pained by each additional mile I have to keep him caged,
the turnoff I am seeking endlessly delaying its appearance,
then, when reached, leading only to another tedious stretch
before I arrive at my destination, his former residence,
a Forgotten Felines foster home.

Cramped, smelly, it's a dump to be sure, but a kind one
in its freedom from our fastidiousness, offering shelter
not only to who knows how many cats, but also to
an I'll-stand-blocking-your-way- till-hell-freezes-over-
if-you-don't-pet-me-dog, and even
to an exotic goat, penned outside.

Having returned Kato to this cocoon of caring, I feel a bit better,
and set my face homeward. But , damned if I'm going
to do a reprise of 6, I improvise an alternate route of return,
heading south, till I hit 118, then east onto 202. Suddenly,
I remember this is the road the poet laureate
once lived on. His invitation list at one time included us]
for gourmet parties, free-flowing wine, jazz always on tap,
each occasion floated on the wit of the host.
But he seems to have moved, his home—
I can barely identify it—
become just another house in the burbs.

And now I turn onto Route 100, the road I lived just off
of for so many years, the road whose nice round number
had given me such pleasure , and I hit the wonderful stretch
of it running unchecked alongside the reservoir
that always tugged my head to the side as I drove
(who can resist looking at water?) and does so once again.
But—let's be real— the road now sits draped
in an undeniable if invisible, time-woven shroud.
It is no longer "mine."
Should I stop the car, get out, sink to the shoulder,
let the tears come , and one day say:
"By the waters of Westchester I sat down and wept"?
I keep going.

I continue beyond my turn-off point, and here comes,
as I knew it would, oh God,
my old farmhouse on Colonial Hill, partly,
teasingly as ever, obscured behind trees,
but now plainly sporting a knockout addition,
my sweet, small, eccentric abode turned
into a stranger's demi-mansion.

What a rocky ride this has been: the cat gone,
the parties gone, the road gone, the house gone.
I must tag each of these parts, and so many others
on the moving dis-assembly line of my life,
with the shimmering song-line delivered
in great Roy Orbison's weird, wafting soprano:
"I'm CRYing, CRYing, CRying, oooooover youuu."

THE CHOICE

I'll take the night any day
over the terrible power of twilight,
the irrevocably undone
over the inexorable undoing,
the bleak safety of the gone
over the pain of the going,
the light simply remembered
over the sight of it draining away.

CHAIN SAW

Jerked into articulation, you have but
two voices: idling, a sullen, muttering gargle,
at work, a rasping hysterical scream
as you eagerly sink your teeth
into trees both vertical and supine.

You could be considered a friend,
furnishing us with the raw stuff of furniture,
fuel for our fireplaces, enlarged views.
Yet you level our forests,
leaving not even bare, ruined choirs
but only air where late
the richly tangled canopy has been.

O deafening *penis dentatus,*
had you been invented much earlier,
Death might have chosen *you*—
not the silent scythe—as the emblem
of his readiness to cut us all
down to size.

But it might have been better
had you existed only in movies,
had "Chain Saw Massacre"
referred to screams on the screen
and not land laid low.
As it is, we are stuck with you,
one more of our ingenious mistakes.

FROM A BENCH IN RIVER PARK AT TWILIGHT

Seated among variegated plantings,
I watch New Jersey's baby skyline
begin to glow, one building showing
a row of lights mysteriously set
in a diagonal. Sporting a huge helmet,
a boy no older than three skims by
on his scooter. Plugged into an IPod,
a passing, lip-ringed man nods steadily,
his neck a circular frieze of tattoos.
Struggling to carry a large painting,
a long-haired young woman totters
past, wearing platform shoes on steroids.

For a little while, I can think of us
(the human race, I mean), not
as earth's undoers, but its adorners,
ourselves among the decorations.

DUSTING

Dust persists—that's all there is to it.
Wipe the cooktop completely clean of it,
it will be back. It only takes a certain slant of light
to reveal the return. As the Good Book says,
it is what we are made of, as well as what
we go back to. And that goes for all and everything—
Nicole Kidman, starfish, tennis balls,
the Andromeda galaxy, pantyhose.

So whatever those Elizabethans may say
about the eternizing power of poetry,
the pen writing this is dust, held by dust,
putting dust down on dust.
You still want to wield that rag?Go ahead—
don't say you haven't been warned.

SHORT DESCENT

> blue-bleak embers, ah my dear,
> Fall, gall & gash themselves gold-vermilion.
> —Gerard Manley Hopkins

"Embers Falling" is the name of his rock group,
its young leader tells me, his intensity fused
with his American vagueness—"it's something in the Bible,"
he says—that's good enough for him.

I walk away from our talk, snagged by the name,
some tiny enclave of my brain stuck on it.
I bring it to my friend Charles, Biblical scholar,
who comes up empty as far as the Good Book is concerned,
then finds its source in *Knife of Dreams*
by Robert Jordan, purveyor of pop fantasies.

Embers falling—Hopkins has done,
for all time, the crackling outburst of their landing, but what of
their short descent between log and grate, grate
and hearth, en route to splashdown? They are on their own,
if only for a second: flaming, falling, free.

A rock group could do worse for its name.

AH, OF COURSE

Last week I prepared a vegetable
whose name I couldn't recall, so couldn't say,
 that being the real frustration,
wired as we are to turn thought into speech.

Hoping to coax forth the recalcitrant
syllables, I stared hard at the veggie
in question, shaped like a smallish carrot,
but of a sickly pallor far removed
from bold orange, the peel lined and rough,
suggesting hard usage. Did it have to struggle
to mature, so that it could be picked,
peeled, cooked and chewed? And after all that,
could I not come up with its name?

Tonight , a friend is proclaiming
parsnip the most under-appreciated
of vegetables. Ah, of course—
that's what it was, *parsnip*, the word
symmetrically framed by p's
asymmetrically produced, the first
by a puff, the second by a drawing back
and closing of the lips. Ah, the joy
of eating, the joy of saying.

RODEO

Its trees newly endowed with May's
lush foliage, my town's measured,
one-mile path beckons me, and I decide,
though I couldn't tell you why,
that for the duration of my walk,
I will banish from my brain all words
(which is to say, thought, as we usually
think of it), admitting to that normally
verbose organ only sights and sounds
as may occur along the way,
an exercise in pure mindfulness.

Eager to start walking, I have embarked
too lightly dressed, so that
when a short, treeless stretch allows
an unimpeded sun to warm my shoulders,
I am grateful, and think (I can't help it,
the words arrive uninvited), " the sun's
got my back," and further think
that tonight I'll stand on the porch,
look up and say "the moon's
got my front," thereby completing
a symmetrical relationship to earth's
two most significant others.

But I'm not there yet, I'm still on my walk,
and here comes a group of men
having the vulnerable, slightly lost
look of the mentally challenged,
and I think (there I go again) "what kind
of words do they command, is theirs
a deprived language, full of empty spaces?"
And I further think "what was I thinking

when I decided to exclude words
from my mind, however briefly?"

Words allow us to ride
our bucking world,
if only in spurts,
lasso it before it gets
completely away,
and sometimes, too,
gallop beyond
its field of gravity.

Go, cowboy, go.

INTRUDER

Who is this intruding upon the twilight,
sun subtly settling itself into whatever lies
below the horizon, airplane softly gargling
in the distance, scattering of birds routinely
getting their obscure last words out before being
shooshed by the impending darkness?

It is yours truly, huffing and puffing,
straining to squeeze in a last-minute
aerobic jog, work up a sweat,
struggle against the countdown
to death—marked by one more day
being crossed off his personal calendar—
unable to accept this latest disappearance
without uttering this peep.

OTHER ANAPHORA LITERARY PRESS TITLES

PLJ: Interviews with Best-Selling YA Writers
Editor: Anna Faktorovich

Inversed
By: Jason Holt

Notes on the Road to Now
By: Paul Bellerive

Devouring the Artist
By: Anthony Labriola

100 Years of the Federal Reserve
By: Marie Bussing-Burks

River Bends in Time
By: Glen A. Mazis

Interview with Larry Niven
Editor: Anna Faktorovich

An Adventurous Life
By: Robert Hauptman

CPSIA information can be obtained at www.ICGtesting.com
Printed in the USA
BVOW03s1328210515

401357BV00001B/21/P

9 781937 536862